THE RACE AGAINST JUNK FOOD

Starring

The Snak Posse (**S**uper **N**utritionally **A**ctive **K**ids)

The Adventures in Good Nutrition Series

ILLUSTRATOR   *DENNY FINCKE*
AUTHORS   *ANTHONY BUONO, ROY NEMERSON & BRIAN SILBERMAN*
COLORISTS   *APRIL MOSEN, AIMEE BUONO & DENNY FINCKE*
EDITORS   *DOLORES & ROBERT ORCHANIAN*

"This is the second night in a row these kids are eating fast food," Tommy's Mom says, "they're going to turn into pudgy little piglets if we keep feeding them like this!" Dad has brought home some McTreats again and Mrs. Thompson is not happy with his choice.

2

"C'mon honey!" Tommy's Dad says through a mouthful of food. "This is easy to pick up on the way home and besides, the kids love it." "I don't love it," Tommy blurts out. "I'm sick of eating this fatty, greasy food!"

For a moment, Tommy feels as if he is floating in space. Then suddenly, he feels like he is being thrown onto a super fast roller coaster ride. He looks around and realizes that he is tumbling down a huge slide with great big letters attached to it.

"Calling ahead to his new orange friend, Tommy asks, "What is this, an alphabet lesson? I learned my ABCs years ago!" "No, you're on the Vitamin Highway!" the mysterious orange boy yells back. "The road to Freshworld, the land of good nutrition. C'mon we've got to keep moving! Just don't make any wrong turns."

Mushrooms
Avocados
Prunes
Spinach
Broccoli

Artichokes
Asparagus
Corn, Peas
Beans

When the vitamin highway comes to an end, Tommy falls straight on his head into a field of soft, green grass.

He shakes the cobwebs from his head and tries to get a better look. Tommy is astounded by what he sees in front of him.

"Has the whole world turned into fruits and vegetables? What is this place?" Tommy asks out loud. "You're in Freshworld, Tommy," comes that same voice again, " and my name is Flash Carotene."

Tommy turns around to see a boy sitting on a branch above him. "Hey, carrot kid!" Tommy says, "Why am I here and how do you know my name?"

"Wow, you sure ask a lot of questions," Flash Carotene says. "You're here because I need your help for the big relay race. All of us do. All of Freshworld needs your help...Why don't you follow me to meet the rest of my friends. We're called the **Snak** Posse, **S**uper **N**utritionally **A**ctive **K**ids. We'll tell you everything you need to know!"

Flash and Tommy race down the hill to town. "This place is fantastic!" Tommy shouts. "It's so alive and everyone is so happy!" "That's why it's called Freshworld and the Snak Posse want to keep it that way," Flash says. "It's also why we have to race the Sugar Coat Gang. They're a bad bunch who have just moved into town. All they do is eat junk food, smoke cigarettes and just mess things up!"

All around the healthy looking citizens of Freshworld are bursting with energy. Flash suddenly points. "Look, there's Blush, skipping rope. Hey, Blush, have you seen Silky Stalk?" "She's playing basketball," Blush calls out between hard breaths. "Blush looks like a tomato!" Tommy says. "Maybe because she is one," Flash replies, laughing.

11

Suddenly, a yellow streak comes dashing around the corner. It's Banana Bolt on his roller blades. "Hi, guys," he says, braking to a halt. "I've been behind enemy lines. The word is that the Sugar Coat Gang is preparing booby traps to beat us." "No way," shouts Kernel. "What kind of tricks could they come up with anyway?"

Suddenly a voice from above yells down at the Snak Posse.
"Hey! Fungus among us!" Startled, the whole group looks
up to see balloons heading straight at them.

The Snak Posse are suddenly covered in sticky, gooey
stuff. "Hope you guys didn't shower yet! Ha! Ha! Ha!"

15

The Sugar Coat Gang roars with laughter from their stinky, flying bathtub. "Bulls eye!" Chip screams. "Yeah! The Sugar Coat Gang strikes again!" Big Cheese yells. "Those veggie nerds don't know what they're getting into racing us. They're going to get destroyed!"

The Sugar Coat Gang knows there is no way they can beat the Snak Posse in a fair and square relay race, so they plan ways to cheat. "I want to get Blush!" the Twicks Twins scream together. "Maybe we can grease up the rope in the climbing contest. She'll slip and fall flat on her tomato head. Yeah, SQUISH!, then we'll use her for ketchup."

After the Snak Posse clean themselves up, Flash Carotene, the captain of the team stands up. "Let's go over our plans one more time. Silky Stalk, since you have been practicing running so hard, you start us off with the 2-mile run. Banana Bolt, you just built a boat, so you compete in the boat race! Blush, you have strong arms and legs from skipping rope, so you do the rope climb. I've been spending time studying the mountain trail, so I'll ride in the Mountain Bike Race."

"And Tommy, since you're the fastest kid in school, you'll finish by running the 50 yard dash. All the good people of Freshworld are depending on you." "I won't let you down," Tommy says somewhat nervously, while stretching his leg muscles.

On the day of the race, Mayor Strawberry is standing at the podium. He announces in a loud, echoing voice, "This relay race will prove once and for all whether eating healthy food is cool or if junk food is better! The winners will be the heroes of Freshworld. The losers have to leave town forever... On my right are our friends, the Snak Posse and Tommy. On my left is the Sugar Coat Gang."

The race is about to begin. The Sugar Coat Gang stands around eating donuts and drinking soda. The Snak Posse stretch their muscles to warm up. They eat oranges for extra energy and drink water. Silky Stalk turns to talk to Trixie. "You're not going to make it halfway through the race if you guys keep eating like that." "Don't you worry about what we do, Veggie kid," Trixie snaps back. "You better worry about how you're gonna win this race. Ha! Ha! Ha!"

Excitement and loud cheering fill the air. Who will be the champions of Freshworld and who has to leave town? Will the townspeople stay healthy or will they turn to junk food and be like the Sugar Coat Gang? The Mayor waves a white flag and announces, "ON YOUR MARKS..., GET SET..., GO!" Instantly, Silky leaps out ahead.

Confidently, Silky widens her lead as she leaves Trixie in the dust. She begins to wonder if Trixie is still in the race.

As Silky Stalk turns around to check, she doesn't see Dixie, Trixie's twin sister, leap in front of her. "Hey, how did you do that!" Silky yells ahead.

HUFF PUFF

"Silky, where have you been!?" Bolt asks. "They're cheating," Silky says when she finally reaches him. "What else would you expect from the Sugar Coat Gang," Banana Bolt replies. "Don't worry, I'll take care of them. No one gets the slip on this Banana."

Bolt starts paddling his Banana Boat with all his power, but he doesn't move an inch! "I'm not getting anywhere. That greasy Chip is going to cream me!" he says. "That's because they've hooked your boat!" Silky Stalk shouts.

Silky quickly sets Bolt's boat free. "Have a nice trip", Dixie says as she falls over with laughter. Silky gives Dixie an angry look as Bolt speeds away.

Banana Bolt uses all his energy to catch Chip who sweats and wheezes with every stroke of his paddle. "See you later and I'm a chip hater!" Bolt yells as he passes Chip.

Just as Banana Bolt says this, Chip presses the bubble button on his boat. He blasts ahead of Bolt on a stream of air bubbles. Bolt is shocked as he watches Chip speed away without using his oar.

Blush is waiting at the cliff for Banana Bolt, so she can start the rope climbing contest.   By the time Bolt gets there, Baby Runt is halfway up even though his arms and legs are not moving.

Blush catches up to Baby Runt quite easily, but every time she tries to pass, he blows smoke in her face and she slips down the rope.

When Blush finally stops coughing, she looks up to see Baby Runt finishing the climb. "Why is that baby able to climb so fast?" she asks herself... She can't see two Camels hiding behind some carrots and broccoli pulling up Baby Runt's rope.

A tired Blush gathers all her strength. With a final burst of energy, she climbs the rest of the rope reaching the top just in time to see Baby Runt tag Big Cheese. Big Cheese takes off onto the trail.

"Blush, you smell like an ashtray. What happened?" Flash asks. "Sorry, Flash," says a tired Blush, finally arriving . "They're using all these tricks… I'm so upset…" "Don't worry," Flash Carotene responds. "They're not the only ones who know a few tricks. Just watch."

25

Pedaling as fast as he can, Flash Carotene aims his bike onto a big rock in the hill, using it as a launch pad. His bike takes off like a rocket, soaring over Big Cheese. "See!?" says Flash, looking back at the Big Cheese. "Sometimes the best trick is just being extra good at what you do! Later, Big Cheese!"

Flash is so sure he is going to win that he doesn't see the next booby trap. PLOP!!! Flash Carotene crashes into a gooey, chocolate syrup bog. "Enjoying your bath?" laughs the Camel from behind a bush.

Flash uses all his might to pull himself and his bike from the gooey trap set by the camel. "I'm not worried," Flash replies. "When this race is over, we'll be the ones laughing." Determined not to lose, he gets on his bike and races to catch Big Cheese.

As Flash is pulling even with Big Cheese, another Camel sneaks up behind Tommy and begins to tie his shoe laces together, while Sweetheart smiles, offering candy. "Let's be friends, Darlin'," she says batting her eyes. "Here, eat some of these. They're delicious." "No way!" Tommy says, waving his hands.

Flash and the Big Cheese reach Tommy and Sweetheart at the same time. The final event to decide the winner is about to begin. The race is all even! "Flash, you made it. Now watch me go!" Tommy says excitedly.

Tommy doesn't realize he's been tricked. As he turns to run, his laces tighten and he crashes to the ground. "Bye, Darlin'," Sweetheart says, running off as her body tips from side to side. Tommy is stunned!

As Tommy looks up, he sees that Sweetheart is on her way to winning the race. Tommy doesn't have any idea how he could catch up to Sweetheart in such a short race!

"Tommy, how does it feel to be a loser?" a reporter asks. "It seems that Sweetheart will win the race for the Sugar Coat Gang. Because of you, Tommy, Freshworld will soon become Junkworld!" The Snak Posse rush to help Tommy. "Don't give up!" they tell him.

The Snak Posse hold hands, forming a circle around Tommy. They all say, "Tommy needs the POWER OF FIVE! THE POWER OF FIVE FRUITS AND VEGETABLES!" As the sun shines brightly from above, a rainbow of color bathes Tommy with energy. Tommy springs to his feet, amidst cheering and chanting. "Tommy… Tommy… Tommy!!!"

Tommy's body now pulses with the power of nature's vitamins and nutrients. Every muscle in his body feels strong. He runs faster than ever before! Any booby trap that the Sugar Coat Gang have waiting, will be no match for Tommy.

Looking ahead, Tommy sees the Twicks sisters. They're squirting huge gobs of ketchup and mayonnaise onto the track ahead of him. Tommy leaps as high as he can into the air. He lands in the middle of the gob with such force it splatters all over the Twicks sisters. Tommy keeps running.

31

Next, Tommy sees that Chip and Baby Runt have built a huge wall made out of hamburgers right in the middle of the track. Tommy raises his arms to his head turning himself into a battering ram. He crashes through the wall with such force that Chip and Baby Runt are pounded on the head with their own hamburgers.

Finally, Tommy sees that a Camel goon has built a machine made of giant cigarettes. It's blowing a tremendous cloud of smoke right at Tommy. With all his might, he blows the smoke right back into the Camel's face, leaving him choking. "We'll get you yet, cough, cough, if it's the last thing that we do," the Camel says.

Tommy has passed the Sugar Coat Gang's last trick, but Sweetheart is still ahead and nearing the finish line. Tommy races, never giving up. He notices that she is struggling with every step. Then, right before the finish line, she faints from exhaustion. "I guess that was one candy too many, Sweetheart!" Tommy screams as he crosses the finish line and wins the race for the Snak Posse and all the people of Freshworld.

"Great job, Tommy. You helped us save Freshworld from the Sugar Coat Gang. Now, all the townspeople will be convinced that good food and exercise are awesome. Go get your family and come back for the best victory party ever."

"Hey, you guys will never believe where I just came from," Tommy shouts as he pops out of the fruit bowl. "It's called Freshworld and you're all invited back!"

35

At the victory picnic back in Freshworld there is fun and excitement everywhere. People are dancing, playing games and eating lots of great tasting, healthy food. Sergeant Pepper's Lonely Artichoke Heart Band is playing some cool music. Everybody is having a great time. The Sugar Coat Gang, having lost the relay race, is leaving Freshworld. Garbage pails are stuffed with junk food like candy bars, potato chips and soda that nobody wants. "Now get out and stay out of town," the people yell as the Sugar Coat Gang fly off in their bathtub.

36

Back at home…"Hey kids, look at what Dad just brought home to eat!" Mrs. Thompson says.

"It took a trip to FreshWorld for my Dad to discover what kids like you and me already knew. When you want something that tastes great and gives you extra energy, FRUITS AND VEGGIES ARE AWESOME!"

The End